KAMALA

HARRIS

Table of Contents

Introduction

Kamala Harris first gained sustained national attention as a Democratic Party presidential candidate in 2020. However, she has been a public servant for most of her professional life, beginning in 1990. Born in Oakland, California, much of her inspiration came from the political turmoil and civil unrest that was on the news most nights as she grew up. It influenced her life directly as she was the daughter of a woman who moved to the United States from India and a father who moved to the United States from Jamaica. Both of her parents moved to the United States to pursue greater opportunities, and the paths of both of her parents helped to shape Kamala to become the person she is today. Her parents divorced when she was young, and her mother moved several times to continue her cancer research work. Harris went with her mother and sister to India to visit her family on her mother's side, and she visited her father's family in Jamaica. She and her mother and sister also lived in Canada for a few years, so the young Kamala learned to speak several languages.

Harris seemed to take a particular interest in justice and inequality, and she studied economics and political science. After graduating from Howard University in Washington DC, Harris went to UC Hastings College of the Law in San Francisco to earn her law degree. She graduated in 1989 and quickly got a position as the deputy district attorney in Oakland, where she served from 1990 to 1998. During this time, she earned a reputation for being tough on crime. Harris did have some of the more challenging criminal cases as she prosecuted primarily cases related to drug trafficking, gang violence, and sexual abuse. In 2004, her formidable reputation helped her become the District Attorney of San Francisco, then, in 2010, the Attorney General of California. She was elected to a United States Senate seat in 2016, and she entered the Senate as the junior California Senator in 2017. Her reputation for being an adept and tenacious questioner continued during her time in the Senate. During her first term, she served on several important committees, including select committees on Homeland Security and Government Affairs, Intelligence, Judiciary, and the Senate Budget.

Many of the positions she has held have been marked as firsts – first woman, first African American, and first American of Indian descent. This continued when, in 2020, she was chosen by Joseph Biden to be his running mate as the Democratic Vice Presidential Nominee. She was not the first woman to be selected as the vice-presidential candidate, but she is the first African American to be one of the two main parties' vice presidential nominee, and the first person of Indian descent to be on the ticket for either of the two parties.

Chapter 1

Early Life

Born on October 20, 1964, Kamala Devi Harris was the oldest child of two adults who had immigrated to the United States. Her parents had excelled in education; her father, Donald Harris, at the University College of the West Indies in Jamaica, and her mother, Shyamala Gopalan, at the University of Delhi in India. Each of them had aspirations that led them to emigrate to America, where they had both been accepted to the University of California, Berkeley. Instead of meeting in classes (Gopalan was studying for her doctorate in nutrition and endocrinology; Harris was working toward a doctorate in economics), the pair met and fell in love during the civic upheaval of the Civil Rights Movement. Having met at protests, they were both passionate about racial equality in the United States. They had come to America for the education, but they stayed because of their passion for politics and a growing love for each other. They married before graduating from college, and Kamala Harris was born in Oakland.

Despite having a child, both her parents remained active in racial activism. This was the type of family that Kamala Harris grew up in for the first few years of her life. She was taken to protests in her stroller and may have been there when her mother met the Reverend Martin Luther King, Jr. Her mother took her to India to see family members. Her maternal grandfather was a high profile political figure, and her maternal grandmother traveled around to more rural areas to teach girls and young women about childbirth. She also visited her father's family in Jamaica as a child, though this part of her history does not get as much attention, likely because she spent more time with her mother.

When her father was offered a job as a professor at the University of Wisconsin-Madison, the couple separated. In 1971, Gopalan started divorce proceedings. Harris was only seven at the time. Two years later, Gopalan was granted custody of both daughters. Kamala and Maya spent their summers and holidays visiting their father, but their mother was their primary parent, playing a much larger role in their lives.

Her mother moved them into a duplex in a poverty-stricken part of Southwest Berkeley.

During this time, the practice of busing was used to desegregate schools. This meant that Kamala took a bus a longer distance to go to a better school where she could get a better education.

While getting a better education through the short-lived bussing program, both girls received an even more inspiring education in their mother's lab. She often put them to work cleaning up test tubes. Whenever she had to travel for work, the two girls were left with a daycare that provided additional education about notable African Americans in history. It has been said that Kamala learned about George Washington Carver before she learned about President George Washington. While they were half Indian American, they looked African American. Aware of how they would be perceived by many in the United States, Gopalan made sure they had a better understanding of how instrumental African Americans had been throughout American history. Gopalan did this to help make her daughters more confident in a country that had long suffered the scourge of racism.

Harris has discussed seeing how her mother was treated, not only because she was an immigrant, but also because she was a woman.

Like the time when Gopalan was passed over for a professorship at Berkeley in favor of a man with far fewer qualifications. Harris herself says that she remembers times where her mother was "treated as though she were dumb because of her accent."

Eventually, Gopalan was offered a position at McGill University in Montreal, Canada, a position she accepted. This was only one of several moves the mother and her two daughters made. After a few years, Gopalan and her little family ended up back in Berkeley. Part of the reason she was able to be so mobile was because she was a primary researcher on breast cancer. Her coworkers remember Gopalan often speaking out against racial bias, especially when it was directed toward any of the students she was mentoring.

Though not nearly as present in their lives, Kamala's father also showed them that an African American could gain recognition. He was the only African American professor in the Stanford University economics department in 1972 and one of only a few black professors at Stanford. Initially, he was only supposed to teach at the school for two years, but in that time, he had become such a popular professor with the students that they became dissatisfied that he was being forced to leave. He had taught a different type of economics that forced them to think differently. Because of the students' outrage, the school hired him as a full-time professor in 1975. The people who have worked with him have said that the way Kamala questioned presidential appointees during her time in the Senate was very similar to how her father used to question students in his class.

Both Kamala and her sister Maya gained a greater understanding of their potential by watching their very dedicated and outspoken parents. Even divorce was not something that could mar their potential. This gave Harris a strong background in better understanding the world of higher education and how her race and gender could be used against her if she let them.

Chapter 2

The World During Her Early Life

Kamala often cites her early formative years as a significant influence over the direction her life took. The fight for their rights that brought her parents together was not a fight just in the Bay Area where she was born, but worldwide. Life was changing and shifting in unpredictable ways. Though born at the end of the Baby Boomer generation, Harris still was alive for many of the most notable events of that generation. She was four years old when the Reverend Martin Luther King, Jr. was killed. She was five years old when Neil Armstrong walked on the moon.

The Vietnam War was still raging, but the Pentagon Papers, released in 1971, started to turn public opinion against the war when Americans learned that several administrations had lied to them. She was just ten years old when President Richard Nixon was forced to resign over the Watergate scandal. The next year Saigon fell, ending the US involvement in Vietnam.

Technology was rapidly changing the way people did things. Two Concorde jets flew out of Europe, revolutionizing how people traveled by air. The massive computers or highly specialized computers of previous generations were being increasingly shrunk, and the hardware worked far more efficiently, giving rise to the possibility of computers being used at work, then eventually a part of the home life. Although it would be more than a decade before it entered homes, the Internet was born while she was still young. Most computers could not handle the Internet, and it was nothing like what it is today, but it was still present. Email is a bit older, as the first one was sent back in 1971 by Ray Tomlinson. The email was not terribly interesting as it was mostly a test, but it was still the first email. It did not gain much attention, though, as most people had no idea what email was, and most people did not know how to operate a computer in the 1970s.

She was not yet 20 years old when the AIDS epidemic began to attract a great deal of attention in the United States and worldwide. When she was only 20, thousands of people back in her mother's native country, India, died because of an industrial disaster that poisoned them. It is estimated that 15,000 Indians in the area around where the disaster occurred died, and children born in the region today are still suffering from congenital disabilities due to the accident.

The first 20 years of her life were a period of extreme change, both for the better and for worse. The first tentative steps to establishing a relationship with both China and the Soviet Union occurred in her early life, showing just what can be done with the right diplomatic approach. However, inequality was also continuing to make life difficult for many people around the world.

Chapter 3

Political Activism and College Years

When she was just 13 years old and still living with her mother in Montreal, Kamala lived in an apartment where children were not allowed to play out on the front lawn. Both Kamala and Maya led a demonstration to fight against this rule as there really was not anywhere better for children in the apartment to play. They were successful in their fight, and the ban on children's play was successfully eliminated. This was the start of her long political career.

By the time she finished high school, Harris was back in California. She opted to go to one of the historically black colleges, Howard University. This meant moving to Washington, DC, to attend class. She chose to pursue degrees in both economics (like her father) and political science. During her time at the university, she joined a sorority, Alpha Kappa Alpha. She earned her degree in 1986 but decided to pursue law. She then moved back to San Francisco to attend law school at UC Hastings College of the Law. She returned to living with her mother, sister, and young niece. She has recounted how she attended school, where the environment was tough because people were mainly competing with each other. Then when she returned home, she helped to teach her little niece how to use the toilet. The difference between the two worlds of home and law school helped her learn how to see things from different perspectives. As if that was not enough, she also became President of the Black Law Student Association for Hastings. Despite the difficulty of the competitive nature of getting a law degree at Hastings College of Law, Harris earned her degree in 1989. She quickly moved on to take the California Bar exam and passed it in 1990. With her formal education complete, Harris stepped out to begin her career path.

Chapter 4

Work for District Attorneys

Because she had been exposed to a wide variety of ways that systems could be changed, after Harris passed the California bar, she considered many options for the best way to start making a difference, just like her parents. Her choice was completely different from the one that was expected. In 1990 her first job was as a deputy district attorney for Alameda County in Oakland, California. Her initial cases focused on sexual assaults and other serious crimes. Over time, she also worked on other difficult cases, including gang-related crimes, drug crimes, other types of assaults, and murder.

Initially, her family questioned her decision to be a prosecutor because, while every district attorney's office is different, they are often perceived to be unfairly tough on poor minorities. This lousy reputation made Harris's family very skeptical of her choice in careers. According to Harris, she wanted to start making changes to the system from within. Her grandfather back in

India was a notable politician, and while he had not done anything that was exactly comparable to her job, he had shown that change was possible by being within the system. By contrast, both of her parents worked in niche fields in the private sector and worked for change from outside the system.

In 1994, Harris began dating Willie Brown, the speaker of the California State Assembly. He appointed her to a position on the California Unemployment Insurance Appeals Board and, later, to the Medical Assistance Commission - appointments that were widely criticized at the time. She served in these positions while still working as the deputy district attorney, and records indicate that she earned an additional $80,000 due to these appointments.

In 1995, Brown ran to be the Mayor of San Francisco. Before he won the election, the two broke up, and there are mixed reports on exactly what happened. It seemed that both agreed that the relationship had no real future. This relationship would come back to cause her problems when she started to aspire to higher offices, but, at the time, it only meant that those who thought they would marry were disappointed.

A few years later, the San Francisco District Attorney's office seems to have actively recruited her to work for them around 1998. One of her former colleagues had made the change to work there and sought to bring her over because of her record. Once in San Francisco, Harris continued to work many of the more difficult cases, particularly focusing on teenage prostitution. Historically, the system has treated teen prostitutes as criminals. However, girls who end up in prostitution so early often come from broken homes, were abused, or have some other circumstances that leave them with few real options. Harris pushed to have these young women treated as victims, trying to improve their circumstances. She was tough on cases that involved serial felons. In 2000, she became the head of the San Francisco City Attorney's Division on Families and Children, a position which she held for three years.

While living in San Francisco, Harris began to foster relationships with some influential people in California. This helped to set her up for a much larger role in California politics. Her network of friends included some influential people with money who ultimately backed her during her first campaign.

Chapter 5

First Campaign and Challenges

In 2003, Harris first ran for an elected position when she entered the race for San Francisco's District Attorney. She had been working in a district attorney's office since she had passed the bar 13 years earlier. Her long history in the office, coupled with her influential friends from San Francisco, made her look like an ideal choice on paper. However, running for office is often about more than a person's record, and even with the backing of influential people, she faced an uphill battle to win the election. Perhaps her greatest obstacle was the fact that she was running against an incumbent with whom she had worked: her former boss, Terence Hallinan. She needed to distinguish herself from her former boss, which was not going to be easy to do.

According to someone who worked with her during her first campaign, she worked to communicate that she was just as progressive as her former boss, but that she and her people would be able to more effectively and competently enact the changes that people wanted.

During that first election, she and her former boss ended up close enough to need a runoff. Harris was able to win the runoff, getting 56.5% of the counted votes. This was the first time Harris gained the distinction of firsts in a long line of firsts. She was the first African American to serve as the district attorney in the entire state of California.

That same year, another up-and-coming Democratic won his first seat. Gavin Newsom was elected to become the new Mayor of San Francisco. During this time, Harris and Newsom became close friends, and they continued to support each other as they moved up in state politics. Meanwhile, Harris got to work trying to change the system from the inside.

Chapter 6

San Francisco's District Attorney

Harris's record during her time as San Francisco's District Attorney is much harder to define because the choices made by a politician are scrutinized much more closely than those who are not elected to their positions.

Harris ran as a progressive in San Fransisco - one of the most liberal cities in the United States. To prove that her former boss was less competent than Harris promised to be, she pointed out that the city had a low felony conviction rate. Hallinan pointed to the reforms that he had implemented and to the liberal jury pools as the reason why the felony conviction rate in San Francisco was far lower than almost any other part of the state. He had expanded some services and started several initiatives intended to rehabilitate inmates and reduce recidivism rates. Those convicted of minor drug charges were offered ways of getting clean and receiving help for their problems instead of labeling them as criminals - similar to what Kamala had done for teenage prostitutes.

Harris used this against him, though, framing herself as progressive but tough on crime. Some of her critics suggested that her being "tough on crime" was antithetical to what her parents had fought for several decades earlier since the "tough on crime" approach so often disproportionately targets and harms poor minorities.

Just a few months after taking office, Harris stuck to one of her primary promises of being against the death penalty when it was put to the test after on officer in the police department was shot and killed. As the district attorney, she refused to put the death penalty on the table for the perpetrator. This drew much ire from the police and other politicians, most notably Dianne Feinstein, who would later serve with Harris as a Senator from California. In her eulogy to the fallen police officer, Feinstein openly criticized Harris for her refusal to call for the death penalty. The other police officers present seemed to agree as they gave Feinstein a standing ovation for the political move. It established an initially contentious relationship between Harris and the police department on whom her office relied for evidence and solving cases. It took her a decade to repair the damage from this apparent miscalculation of doing what she had promised to do when she ran for district attorney.

Despite this early controversy, she won a second term. Toward the end of her time as the city's district attorney, Harris found her office embroiled in another scandal because it was discovered that one of the technicians in her office had been stealing cocaine from the crime lab. As a result, all of the evidence was compromised, and many cases had to be dismissed.

It was the San Francisco Police Department that was responsible for the operation of the lab, not the district attorney's office. It was also a problem that occurred before she assumed the office. The problem was not that the theft had occurred, but with the way that Harris handled it. Since the district attorney's office did not notify the defense attorneys, this was a Constitutional violation of the rights of the affected defendants. The case went to the San Francisco Superior Court, and the ruling was handed down in 2010 that, by failing to disclose the problem, the people "at the highest levels of the district attorney's office knew that Madden was not a dependable witness at trial and that there were serious concerns regarding the crime lab." Madden was the drug lab technician who had taken the cocaine from the lab.

In 2008, Harris refused to help defend Proposition 8, which had banned same-sex marriage in California. As the district attorney in the American city with the most openly gay residents, it would have been both highly unpopular for her to enforce this law and not a clear representation of the people she was meant to serve. The ruling was overturned a few years later.

In an effort to reduce truancy in schools, she also supported a measure that made parents criminally responsible when their children missed too many days of school. The result was a drop in truancy in San Francisco, and she later pointed to the measure as a successful way of reducing truancy rates when she ran for office as the Attorney General of California. However, she has since expressed regret for the policy that disproportionately affects low-income minorities.

Chapter 7

Criticisms

As a public figure from the beginning of her career, Harris has been subject to a wealth of criticism. Whether or not each of these criticisms is earned is debatable since public figures are put to far more scrutiny than people in the general public. Any connection to issues or problems or people who create problems stains a politician's reputation, not always deservedly.

As California is considered a progressive state and San Francisco is famously among the most liberal cities in the state, Harris's record as the district attorney for the city has been viewed as far less liberal or progressive than that of her former boss. Where he had pushed for reforms and rehabilitation, Harris supported moves that made actions criminal that had not been before, with the truancy measure being one of the most notable examples. Many felt that the punishments were far too punitive for the offense, placing an even greater burden on those who were struggling.

What Harris's campaign had failed to point out was that her predecessor's low conviction rate did not mean that he had been an ineffective district attorney. Again, the low conviction rate was, in part, due to factors beyond his control. During his time in office, Hallinan had helped reduce the number of violent crimes within the city by 60%. By comparing a low conviction rate to crime running rampant, the campaign misrepresented what Hallinan's office had actually achieved. Harris also used scare tactics to sway voters, using the image of someone with tattoos holding a gun and appearing to make a gang sign while declaring that "Enough is enough!" on the mail-out campaign. The violent crimes suggested by the image were actually in decline, and not on the rise. Harris' progressive critics to the left of her have sometimes accused her of misleadingly painting herself as a progressive while her campaign had helped remove a far more progressive candidate.

One of the biggest criticisms of her time as the San Francisco District Attorney comes from the progressives who feel that she ended up pandering more to the big money that had helped to get her elected. She seemed to have spent most of her time in San Francisco trying to establish a better relationship with the police following her refusal to push for the death penalty during her first year in office. The fear-mongering tone that she had established for her first campaign followed the trends of the 1990s instead of the more progressive attitude that her predecessor had set for the city. Nonetheless, Harris successfully used her record of being tough on crime to win her next prominent position as California's attorney general.

Chapter 8

Working Toward Reforms

With the most significant criticism of her time in office in San Francisco revolving around her view of the death penalty and her less progressive, more traditional approach to crime, there were not nearly as many reforms during her tenure as her predecessor brought about. However, she did indeed implement new reforms. For example, she started a program called Back on Track that sought to funnel young, first-time drug offenders into programs that would give them more options. These young offenders were given the option of an apprenticeship or a training program instead of locking them in prison where they would have far fewer opportunities when they got out of their imprisonment.

She also gained a reputation for compassion toward families who were victims of violent crimes or knew people who had died because of these crimes. She kept an open-door policy to offer consolation and support. To ensure that people within her office were more connected to their communities, she required that all deputy district attorneys spend time out in the community. This was not only meant to help make them more recognizable within the community but to make her people have a better understanding of the communities they served. It is challenging to represent people when politicians do not interact with them.

Harris had already proved that she was against the death penalty. Despite the criticism she received during her first year, Harris did stand by what she had said while running for office. She did not believe in the death penalty, so she was not going to push for it, not even to make exceptions when it would have been easier to do so.

Despite the early problems with the police, she was known as being someone who was very much a "law and order" prosecutor. By the nature of their job, district attorneys work closely with law enforcement. This was why her family had been skeptical of her choice of careers. While her record has been less progressive than several other people to hold the position in the city, she did work toward reforming how younger people were treated by the system. For some, this does not go far enough, while others see it as giving criminals a chance to offend again. Perspective is everything. During most of her time working in San Francisco, Harris tried to improve the lives of the young instead of having them enter into the prison system that would, statistically, ensure they would not be reformed. It is her time working in San Francisco that is often pointed to a reason why she is problematic. In reality, her record shows a willingness to find new solutions when she is shown why it is needed. Her opinion on some issues did change over time, and her ideas have evolved.

Chapter 9

California's Attorney General

In 2010, Harris launched her campaign to become California's attorney general. Her opponent was a Republican from Los Angeles. Regardless of her record as the San Francisco District Attorney (a record that had earned her the name "top cop"), she was portrayed as being too liberal and progressive because of where she served. Her race and gender were also portrayed as being indications that she was liberal, something that was not reflected by her record. The Republican, Steve Cooley, was considered very popular, and many people did not think that she stood a chance of defeating him. She became the state's 32nd attorney general, but the first African American and the first woman to hold the position.

By the end of the election period, the race was so tight that the final results were not ready. Assuming that he had won, Cooley addressed his supporters with a victory speech. Even the San Francisco Chronicle assumed he had won, and they published a story that he had come out on top. It would take three more weeks to finish counting all of the ballots, but by the end, Harris had actually won by 0.8% points.

Like her record in San Francisco, Harris's time as the Attorney General of California made it difficult to portray her as progressive when taking her record into account. She proved popular enough to win her second election, serving for a total of seven years in the position. During both of her campaigns, Donald Trump, and his daughter, Ivanka, donated to her campaigns.

Following the 2008 financial crisis, states were offered mortgage settlements to try to help families. Initially, she was told that her state was being offered $4 billion to alleviate the problems caused by foreclosures. Since California is the most populous state in the union and has the largest gross domestic product of any state (if it were a country on its own, California would rank as the fifth-largest economy in the world, just ahead of India and right behind Germany), she felt that $4 billion was not sufficient for how much the state contributed to the nation. Instead of accepting the offer, she refused to sign until she was able to secure $20 billion to help the homeowners of her state. While some people have accused her of grandstanding, given how much she was able to secure for the state, her move was more than just a stunt. She was able to deliver what she felt was owed to California homeowners.

While she did fight to get Californians more assistance, Harris appeared less inclined to pursue accountability for those who had helped cause the foreclosure problems. In 2012, the California Department of Justice had issued a recommendation that she file a civil enforcement action that would hold OneWest Bank accountable for "widespread misconduct" during the foreclosure process. This was seen as more than just a failing on her part, but a resistance to prosecuting wealthy people to the same extent as she had prosecuted others. One of the people who would have been held accountable was the bank's CEO, Steven Mnuchin, who later went on to become Treasury secretary in the Trump Administration, having been allowed to get away with what some perceive as misconduct in California.

Having spent much time with victims in San Francisco, Harris, by starting Open Justice, made sure that people were able to protect themselves from known criminals. This was an online platform that gave the public access to data about the criminal justice system. However, this was not just a way to help learn about crime statistics; it let the public access data about the police. As a result, it helped to make the police more accountable as the memory of the Rodney King beating was still very much on the minds of Californians. The data included the number of people killed or injured while they were in police custody.

However, her record of police accountability is not so clear cut. In both 2014 and 2015, two African American men were shot by police, yet her office was accused of not investigating. This made the reason behind the databases appear far less helpful as there appeared to be little accountability when it mattered. The criticism was further compounded when, in 2015, Harris said she did not support a bill that was in the state assembly that would have required all attorneys general to initiate a process to appoint special prosecutors following the use of deadly force by the police. She received more harsh criticism for initially being opposed to enforcing a law that would have made sure all police had to wear body cameras while on duty, further eroding the belief that she was dedicated to real police reform.

Perhaps the most noticeable difference between her early days in San Francisco and her time as state attorney general was her apparent change of opinion on the death penalty. Two separate initiatives would have banned the death penalty in California, but Harris did not support either of the two initiatives. This move gained her more criticism for not following through on her convictions, though it was not among the primary issues that would cause her problems when she ran to be the 2020 Democratic nominee.

Chapter 10

Controversies

As the attorney general of California, Harris did create a database to track violence in police custody, but some have accused her of being unwilling to act on that data. She has touted her move during her time as the attorney general to make police wear body cameras as being progressive but failed to point out that only the California Department of Justice, who worked for her, required cameras. It was not required state-wide, and she explained that requiring body cameras was not a "one-size-fits-all" solution to some of the issues, preferring to leave it up to different regions to decide what was right for them.

Harris' San Fransisco anti-truancy policies continued with her into this role as she pressed for implementing it state-wide. Pointing to San Francisco's reduced numbers of truancy as an example of how the measure was successful, she supported a law that made it illegal for students between kindergarten and 8th grade to miss more than 10% of school days, unless they had a valid excuse. Parents of kids that fell afoul of this requirement faced either a $2,000 fine or a year in jail. Again, Harris' critics have been quick to complain that this law placed undue burdens on families who had no control over their situation or were already in duress.

A more interesting controversy about Harris actually came from President Barack Obama when he called her the best looking attorney general. While he clearly meant it as a compliment, it upset some people for focusing on her gender and looks over her record and abilities. Obama later apologized for the faux pas. Little has been said about how she received the awkward compliment, but, given some of the things that her mother experienced, it is more likely that a compliment on her record or tenacity would have been a much better way of expressing admiration.

It should be noted that being the attorney general of any state is a difficult job. It is a delicate balance between providing legal counsel to the government and pushing for reform. In a state as large, populous, and diverse as California, it is impossible to do this in a way that will not attract criticism, and much of the criticism that Harris has faced has been based on the kinds of concerns that her family likely felt she would face when she first started in the district attorney's office. However, the primary role of the attorney general is to help uphold the law and work closely with the police.

Chapter 11

The Senate

Harris has a flawless campaign history, winning every position for which she has run. In 2016, she ran for the position of California Senator. During the 2012 Democratic National Convention, she gained national attention for her well-spoken address, earning her the reputation for being a rising star in the party. This likely helped to drive her decision to run for the Senate. Since that address, she has married a well-known attorney, Douglas Emhoff. She is his second wife, and he is her first husband. Like her mother, Harris kept her maiden name.

The idea to run for Senate was likely put into her mind by Barbara Boxer, the California Senator who announced her retirement shortly after Harris married. Not long after that, Harris declared her intention of running for Boxer's seat. Before this, there had been some speculation that President Obama had considered her for the Supreme Court, but she has said that she was not interested in taking a seat on the bench. She has held elected positions that were more closely tied to working with the public, not in ruling from the bench.

By 2015, there was a rising call for reforms. After declaring her intention to run for the Senate, Harris quickly added her voice to those calling for a wide range of changes, from immigration and criminal justice to minimum wages and more protection for women. Her opponent was another Democrat, Loretta Sanchez, who had been a representative in Congress for 20 years. It seems that Harris's campaign for the vacant Senate seat was the easiest first campaign she has ever had as it was not even close. She was not only the most likely candidate to succeed; there did not seem to be any question about whether she would win. The predictions proved right, and she was sworn in as the junior senator for California in January 2017. This was the only time when she began an elected position without the distinction of being a first; she was the second African American and the second Asian American woman to take a place in the United States Senate.

Harris soon joined several different committees, including the Select Committee on Intelligence, Senate Budget, Homeland Security and

Governmental Affairs, and the Judiciary Committee. Her experience as a prosecutor soon showed how well she applied her skills on the committees as she grilled people who were brought before those committees.

Harris had also been working on a book of memoirs called *The Truths We Hold: An American Journey,* published in early 2019. Although the book is written from her perspective, so it should be taken with a grain of salt in terms of the facts (it is impossible to write memoirs without a bias), it does cover the world as she has seen it. The book includes some of her regrets and reflections on her own record. While it is easy to be somewhat cynical, it should be remembered that the best leaders tend to let their views and approaches evolve over time. It shows both growth into a position and an honest reflection on the past to try to do better in the future. All leaders should take the time to assess their own legacy to better understand the main criticisms against them.

Harris followed the template that Obama had set when he was elected to his first term in the Senate. She decided to run for President before her first term was over, less than four years after becoming a senator. However, this did not seem to change the way that she questioned those who came before Congress. Her calculated approach to questioning was established long before her time in the Senate. Harris has been praised for her fairly consistent approach to questioning, regardless of who is in front of her.

Chapter 12

Hard-Nosed Interviewer

Harris, in her different roles within the Senate, reflects her work in the California justice system. She soon earned a reputation for often going on the attack when she disagreed with someone who was appearing in front of Congress. Despite being a new member of the Senate, Harris quickly distinguished herself when the US Attorney General, Jeff Sessions, was called to testify about Russian interference during the 2016 presidential election. At one point, Sessions responded to her persistent questions by saying, "I'm not able to be rushed this fast! It makes me nervous." This is very likely a reflection of how she treated people on the stand as a prosecutor.

However, he was not the first person to sit before her very pressing method of questioning. Just the week before, Harris had asked some very tough questions of Rod Rosenstein in an effort to understand his role in the firing of the then FBI director James Comey, a move that was seen by some as politically motivated. This method of grilling is expected in the courtroom, and is not necessarily a reflection of how the questioner feels about the person in front of them. It is meant to cause the person to really think and respond. The more time a person takes to think, the more time they have to calculate a lie. The rapid-fire questioning often gets a response with less filter that more accurately reflects either the truth or how a person was thinking. This is not always true as some people do not do well when faced with that kind of questioning. Then again, sitting on the stand during a trial, or even in front of Congress, often is not considered a comfortable experience. It is the job of the lawyers or the members of Congress to get the truth, not to ensure that the person is comfortable during the questioning.

Two members of the Senate reprimanded her for being disrespectful during her questioning, Senators John McCain and Richard Burr. They issued reprimands after both of the times when she questioned the people appearing before a committee. When it was pointed out that both men had been equally harsh during the questioning, the two men found themselves having to fight off accusations of being sexist and racist in how they thought she should question others. Since they had not been reprimanded for similar behavior, it is difficult to argue whether different standards were not applied to her. She had only had her seat for a few months, and most junior Senators are not nearly so engaged or so tough during questioning. It is possible that the men expected a less hardline set of questions given how new she was to her position. However, Harris really cannot be blamed for applying the skills she learned as district attorney and attorney general to her approach to questioning people called before Congress. Her ability to question people more thoroughly is one of the reasons that she was a good fit for the position. Committees should be asking hard questions. When a committee takes the time to call people in to talk before them, it is literally the committee's job.

Harris may have gained much attention because of her tough questioning, but it is difficult to argue that she is inconsistent in her approach. She used the same method of questioning for members of the Trump Administration, during the confirmation hearing for Brett Kavanaugh for the vacant seat on the Supreme Court, and even Mark Zuckerberg. Zuckerberg had seemed pretty relaxed up until she began to question him. In April 2018, Congress was looking into data-mining misuse by his company, Facebook, after news broke of some particularly concerning practices by the company. When Harris began questioning, her approach caused Zuckerberg to begin to look uncomfortable as he was not so easily able to brush aside her questions as he had for some of the other Senators.

It is easy to think that her approach changed after she declared her intention of running for the Democratic presidential nominee, but, in truth, her approach was the same as it had been before. Her harsh questioning of US Attorney General William Barr regarding the Robert Mueller report and the 2016 Russian election interference was no less severe as her questioning of Sessions, Kavanaugh, or Zuckerberg.

Chapter 13

Presidential Campaign

When Harris went on *Good Morning America* on January 21, 2019, she announced that she was running for President, making her one of the first to enter the 2020 race. It was Martin Luther King, Jr. Day in the United States, closely tying her campaign with the call for reforms and equality that had been growing in the US for years. She also chose symbolic colors to represent her campaign, yellow, red, and blue. These were the colors associated with Shirley Chisholm, the first African American to run for the US presidency as a member of one of the two major parties.

Within a few months, the field was packed. As the debates started, there were 29 known contenders, and 23 reached the debate stages at some point over the debates. Because of how crowded the field was, the debates were broken up over two nights until enough of the candidates had dropped out to have only one night of debates.

Harris's tactics in questioning were initially used during the debates, gaining her a lot of early attention and support. Her most effective exchange came in the early debates when she directly squared off against the assumed front-runner, Joseph Biden. During this exchange, she brought up his record of being against bussing. Some would argue that she misrepresented his perspective; Biden wanted a better solution than forcing students to go longer distances to get an equal education. The way that Harris framed it made it sound like he was more out of touch with the pulse of the party, a relic of an earlier time who was less interested in advocating for equality. Her attack was effective because she pointed out that his opposition to bussing contradicted her own experience, having been bussed herself. It was the reason why she had received a better education when she went to school. When she was being bussed to schools, Biden was already a Senator, which made her personal story more relatable. Even after this attack, Biden did not seem to hold it against her, even once asking her "to go easy on me, kid" as they shook hands before the beginning of the next debate. Since Harris was friendly with Obama, she and Biden had already been in the same circles long before the debates, so the attacks were not seen as personal; just a part of the job.

There are many reasons given for why Harris's campaign ultimately failed, especially after such early promise. Some point to her campaign's inability to get out a single message to her supporters. The momentum that she gained from her electric performance was not used to further push her ahead in the polls, so she plateaued fairly early in the campaign. Over time, other Democrats moved to the front, and Harris increasingly declined in the polls.

By the end of November 2019, Harris had not seen similar success in the debates or a boost in the polls. She discussed her options with her primary supporters and reached a conclusion. Despite still wanting to run, she simply did not have the funds or the support to continue with her bid for the nomination. On December 3, 2019, she sent an email to those who had supported her campaign, letting them know that she was suspending her campaign. She has said that it was "one of the hardest decisions of my life," and it came after she had spent nearly a full year seeking the candidacy. It was the first time in her history when she failed to gain the necessary support to get the votes for an elected position.

Ironically, there had been much talk during the debates about the electability of the women running for President. They were all said to be less electable than their male counterparts, despite the fact that the women had all been successful for every seat for which they ran. All of the males had failed at least once during their campaigning careers, suggesting that those making the calls were focused on gender as making the women less electable. The evidence to that point suggested that the women were more electable as they all had perfect records, suggesting that they were better able to speak to the needs of the people they represented. If gender was the primary reason, it was not a new problem for Harris as her mother had fought that particular discrimination over most of her life.

Chapter 14

Vice Presidential Candidate

Harris may have dropped out of the running for the Democratic Presidential nominee, but she was still very much in the running to be the vice-presidential nominee. It took her a few months after dropping out of the race, but in early March 2020, she finally endorsed Biden, who was quickly becoming the frontrunner in the shrinking field of presidential candidates. According to her, Harris saw him as the type of candidate who could "unify the people," something that had become seen as nearly impossible as COVID-19 began to spread across America. As even simple safety precautions were seen as politically divisive, the call for a unifier became important to many voters.

When Biden became the presumptive Democratic Nominee, he promised to select a female running mate. Given her strong early performance in the debates, there was much speculation that Harris would be selected. On August 11, he proved them right when he announced that she was his chosen vice presidential running mate.

Harris immediately began receiving criticism, with many Republicans suggesting that she was one of the most liberal senators in the Senate. While she certainly has a much more liberal record, Harris is best classified as a centralist, particularly given the number of actual liberals and progressives who ran to be the Democratic nominee. She was regularly attacked by the other Democrats because of her more traditional record as California's Attorney General.

Harris is currently up for re-election as Senator in 2022. However, if Biden is successful in winning the 2020 Presidential election, the current California Governor Gavin Newsom will be the one to appoint her replacement for the remainder of her term. He will likely discuss the replacement with Harris herself, and there is speculation that she will encourage him to ensure that her potential replacement reflects California's diversity. Though speculation has already begun for this vacancy, it is far too early to be thinking about it. Harris is still a Senator first and running to be vice president second. Should the ticket fail, Harris will continue to serve in her role as a thorough and persistent questioner on many different committees in the United States Senate.

Conclusion

Kamala Harris is the daughter of two immigrants from very different cultures, putting her into a different kind of spotlight than many other politicians. Her father once reprimanded her when she was asked about how she felt about marijuana and she pointed to her Jamaican roots as an indication of how she felt. Her father was displeased that she would perpetuate the Jamaican stereotype as stoners, showing that not all of the criticism leveled against her is entirely biased. Having been raised by two very strong-willed parents, she has learned how to take criticism and to use it to better understand her position.

Her political career has been long and varied and as flawed as any other professional. Like her parents, she has always sought to earn her own legacy, which was nearly undermined by her early relationship with Willie Brown. More recently, when reporters have asked her if she would continue to carry Obama's legacy, Harris was reported to have responded with "I have my own legacy," indicating that she wants to be recognized for her own accomplishments, not as a torchbearer for someone else's.

Ultimately, Kamala Harris takes her mother's inspiring words to heart, "You may be the first, but make sure you're not the last."

Made in the USA
Coppell, TX
07 November 2020

40952455R00031